SCHOLASTIC

NO BORING PRACTICE, PLEASE!

FUNNY FAIRY TALE
GRAMMAR

by Justin McCory Martin

NEW YORK • TORONTO • LONDON • AUCKLAND • SYDNEY
MEXICO CITY • NEW DELHI • HONG KONG • BUENOS AIRES

Teaching *Resources*

To Rex and Donna Martin, my parents,
married 50 years. Fairy tales really do happen.

Scholastic Inc. grants teachers permission to photocopy the reproducible pages from this book for classroom use.
No other part of this publication may be reproduced in whole or in part, or stored in a retrieval system,
or transmitted in any form or by any means, electronic, mechanical, photocopying, recording, or otherwise,
without written permission of the publisher. For information regarding permission, write to
Scholastic Inc., 557 Broadway, New York, NY 10012.

Cover design by Brian LaRossa
Cover and interior illustrations by Mike Moran
Interior design by Sydney Wright

ISBN-13: 978-0-439-58846-1
ISBN-10: 0-439-58846-4
Copyright © 2006 by Justin McCory Martin
Published by Scholastic Inc.
All rights reserved.
Printed in the U.S.A.

1 2 3 4 5 6 7 8 9 10   40   14 13 12 11 10 09 08 07 06

Contents

Grammar Activities

Introduction

For kids, learning the rules of grammar can be a bit like eating green beans. They may know what's good for them, but some dishes just aren't any fun. This book aims to remedy that situation. For example, the prospect of learning to differentiate common, comparative, and superlative adjectives may sound deadly dull to kids. But an exercise in this book called *Fair, Fairer, and Fairest* introduces this concept in a way that's lighthearted and easy to understand.

This book covers topics that are key to honing writing skills: parts of speech, capitalization, plurals, commas, quotation marks, contractions, sentence fragments, homophones, and more. But the rules of grammar have been given what might be called a "fun-over." Inside these pages you'll find a variety of reproducible exercises involving crossword puzzles, letters, invitations, and even an activity called *Pin the Preposition on the Ogre*. The exercises feature amusing takes on familiar fairy tale characters such as Cinderella, fairy tale mainstays such as castles and dragons, as well as fractured fare such as *The Three Microscopic Pigs*.

There are a huge number of grammar rules. Fortunately, there's one rule that can stand just about anyone in good stead most of the time. It goes something like this: *You know good grammar when you see good grammar*. That's actually not a bad test. This book introduces students to the rules of grammar in a way that is memorable and easy to understand. Occasionally, terms such as *predicate* are used, but more often than not this book seeks to teach by example. The aim is to spoon-feed the rules of grammar and make them go down easy. After students have finished this book, they may not remember the term *superlative adjective*. But hopefully they will have learned something far more important—namely, how to use adjectives properly.

So here's wishing your students good grammar. The hope is that this book will make the subject so much fun that kids won't even realize—until it's too late—that they have learned some very useful rules to apply to their writing.

How to Use This Book

This book is broken down into 14 sections by topic such as nouns, adverbs, capitalization, and quotations. Each section begins with a teacher page with helpful information and tips on getting students to think about the main grammar rules that apply to each topic.

One of the best ways to introduce kids to the notion of grammar rules is to break those very rules. On the board, write someone's name without using capital letters. Write a question, but don't use a question mark. You might even try babbling on and on without taking a breath, to produce one long run-on sentence. Then use these examples as springboards to start a discussion about why grammar rules exist and what happens when they're not followed.

The meat of this book is the reproducible activities. They can be used in conjunction with and as a complement to your classroom instruction. They're a great way to provide extra reinforcement for students who need more practice or review before a quiz or test. Designed for flexible use, the activities work well as class work or instant homework. Each reproducible activity also features a "learning extension" to provide further reinforcement of the concept. At the end of the book, you'll find an answer key.

Connections to the Standards

The activities in this book are designed to support you in meeting the following writing standards outlined by Mid-continent Research for Education and Learning (McREL), an organization that collects and synthesizes national and state standards.

Uses the general skills and strategies of the writing process.

- Editing and Publishing: Uses strategies to edit and publish written work (e.g., edits for grammar, punctuation, capitalization, and spelling at a developmentally appropriate level).

Uses grammatical and mechanical conventions in written compositions.

- Uses pronouns in written compositions.
- Uses nouns in written compositions.
- Uses verbs in written compositions.
- Uses adjectives in written compositions.
- Uses adverbs in written compositions.
- Uses coordinating conjunctions in written compositions.
- Uses conventions of spelling in written compositions.
- Uses conventions of capitalization in written compositions.
- Uses conventions of punctuation in written compositions.

Source: *Content Knowledge: A Compendium of Standards and Benchmarks for K–12 Education* (4th ed.). Mid-continent Research for Education and Learning, 2004.

NOUNS

The word *noun* comes from the Latin word *nomen*, which means "name." It's an apt description, because nouns are used to name persons, places, and things. As such, nouns play a starring role in the grammar world. When an action takes place—requiring a verb—that action is done by or to a noun. When a description is used that employs an adjective, that description often applies to a noun.

Here's an exercise you can do in your classroom to demonstrate the importance of nouns. On the board, write: "The Big Bad Wolf huffed and puffed and blew the house down." Then erase the two nouns *wolf* and *house*. Discuss with students how much meaning is lost with the removal of nouns. Invite them to suggest their own sentences, write them on the board, and again, remove the nouns.

Not only are nouns important but they also come in a variety of types including:

✦ common nouns, such as *girl* or *country*;

✦ proper nouns, such as *Cinderella* or the *Land of Oz*;

✦ plural nouns, such as *wizards* or *moats*.

Reproducibles to Reinforce Learning

A great way to introduce students to nouns is the *Wall of Words* exercise (page 7). *The Princess and the Spree* (page 8) helps students get a fix on proper nouns. To teach about the plural forms of nouns, pass out *Give Plurals a Whirl* (page 9).

Wall of Words

Prince Pepper has been imprisoned by Maltrog, the evil sorcerer. The only way to free the prince is to visit the Wall of Words below and use your trusty magic graphite writing device to circle only the nouns. There are 15 of them. Beware: You get only one try. If you make any mistakes, Prince Pepper will be imprisoned forever!

Learning Extension: The 15 nouns in the Wall of Words are great fairy tale vocabulary. Write a tale of your own, using as many of them as you can.

No Boring Practice, Please! Funny Fairy Tale Grammar Scholastic Teaching Resources

7

Name _____ Date _____

The Princess and the Spree

Rewrite the following story, using proper nouns in place of the underlined common nouns.
For example:

Princess Petunia   Omaha
~~The princess~~ was trying to get to ~~the city.~~

The princess was trying to get to the city. She was lost in the forest.

She discovered a trail of food crumbs. She followed the trail, and it led to

a magic car. She turned on the magic car's radio, and a song by a singer

was playing. She began to clap her hands. After she had clapped three

times, the magic car lifted up in the air and flew to the city. It landed in

the parking lot of a store. Perfect! This was exactly where the princess

was trying to go in the

first place. She went inside,

met her friends, and

bought some things.

Learning Extension: Look around. The world is full of proper nouns. Everybody has a name, which is a type of proper noun. Every country, city, park, and street has a name—also proper nouns. Even something simple like your pencil probably has a brand name—once again, a proper noun. So think of some proper nouns that are right around you. Then use them in a modern fairy tale.

No Boring Practice, Please! Funny Fairy Tale Grammar Scholastic Teaching Resources

Name _____   Date _____

Give Plurals a Whirl

There are exceptions, but here are three simple rules for pluralizing nouns:
- Most nouns become plural simply by adding -s. (Example: *toad, toads*)
- To pluralize a noun that ends in *ch, s, sh, x,* or *z,* add -es. (Example: *box, boxes*)
- To pluralize a noun that ends in *y,* replace the *y* with *i* and add -es.
  (Example: *buddy, buddies*)

Now pluralize the following nouns in these fractured fairy tale titles.

1. Goldilocks and the Three Boar_____

2. The Emperor's New Pupp_____ (puppy)

3. Snoring Beaut_____ (beauty)

4. Three Kitty Cat_____ Gruff

5. The Teeny Genie and the Three Small Wish_____

6. Pinocchio's Pepperoni Pizza Part_____ (party)

7. Snow White and the Seven Snowflake_____

8. The Three Huge Hog_____

9. The Wicked Witch_____ of the West

10. One Hundred and One Fox_____

Learning Extension: Pick out a section of a fairy tale and convert all the singular nouns to plural. This is good practice, and it can be pretty fun, too.

VERBS

Without verbs, sentences would be dull and dreary. Verbs provide action and adventure. Here are some examples: *frolic, whirl, grumble, slam, ignite,* and *palpitate.* All these words suggest movement and energy. In fact, a good way to think of verbs is as the engines of a sentence. They're like popping pistons pushing the action along.

Here's a way to get your class thinking about verbs. Draw a picture of a locomotive on the board. Then explain verbs to your students, and ask them to take turns providing examples. Keep a count of their examples. Each verb equals one mile per hour for the locomotive. See how quickly your class can get the train moving at 50 or even 100 miles per hour.

Chances are, students will suggest colorful verbs such as *leap* and *dance.* These are known as action verbs. Explain to them that there's another kind of verb called a linking verb. Some examples of linking verbs are *is, appear,* and *remain.* They are not quite as dramatic as action verbs, but they still have an important job to do. Linking verbs connect the main parts of a sentence (they connect the subject to a predicate noun or a predicate adjective).

Action Verbs	Linking Verbs		
dance	*He*	*is*	*a teacher.*
jump	Subject	linking verb	predicate noun
live			
sleep	*They*	*are*	*glad.*
read	Subject	linking verb	predicate adjective

Of course, it is also important that verbs agree with their subjects. For example, a singular subject requires a singular verb: "The student learns." Likewise, plural subjects require plural verbs: "The students learn."

Reproducibles to Reinforce Learning

Distribute *Lights, Camera, Action!* (page 11) to introduce verbs to students. *Missing Links* (page 12) covers linking verbs, and *Agree to Agree* (page 13) covers subject and verb agreement.

Lights, Camera, Action!

Imagine that you have been asked to direct the action-packed movie *Hot-Rod Pumpkin*. In the script below, replace the underlined verbs with more exciting and specific action verbs.

Cinderella simply had to be home by midnight. She <u>got</u> into her hot-rod pumpkin. The horses, which used to be mice, began to <u>move</u>. The carriage <u>went</u> down the street. It <u>went</u> around a corner.

Soon the pumpkin carriage was <u>going</u> down the highway. Nobody saw the patch of spilled apple juice until they were about to <u>go</u> through it. But these were skillful horses. They quickly <u>went</u> around the apple juice, and the carriage stayed dry. Soon the carriage was <u>going</u> down the road again at full speed.

The horses kept <u>going</u> until they reached Cinderella's home. She <u>got</u> out and <u>went</u> inside. She <u>went</u> through the door just before the clock struck midnight.

Learning Extension: Choose five fabulous action verbs. Use them in sentences or even a short story.

No Boring Practice, Please! Funny Fairy Tale Grammar Scholastic Teaching Resources

11

Name _____   Date _____

Missing Links

Action verbs are exciting verbs such as *holler*, *slide*, or *swoop*. But linking verbs are no less important. As their name suggests, they are used to connect parts of a sentence. Linking verbs connect the subject of a sentence to an adjective or noun. Examples:

Magic wands   are   handy.   She   is   a princess.
Subject   linking verb adjective   Subject linking verb   noun

Select the linking verb in the multiple choice exercises below.

1. The giant _____ huge.
   A) walks   **B)** dresses   **C)** is   **D)** climbs

2. Some princes _____ frogs.
   A) greet   **B)** fight   **C)** examine   **D)** remain

3. The magic lantern's light _____ far away.
   A) seems   **B)** burns   **C)** wiggly   **D)** dances

4. The trolls _____ grumpy.
   A) Ohio   **B)** felt   **C)** happy   **D)** galloped

5. Fortunately, the dragon _____ sleepy.
   A) ate   **B)** likes   **C)** looks   **D)** prefers

6. The porridge _____ bland.
   A) needed   **B)** wanted   **C)** called   **D)** tasted

7. The boy _____ a knight.
   A) became   **B)** insisted   **C)** battled   **D)** found

8. The fairy tale _____ fascinating.
   A) told   **B)** read   **C)** ate   **D)** sounded

Learning Extension: Write a short poem with a fairy tale theme. Use plenty of linking verbs. Here's an example: *The ogre was old. His lair looked cold.*

The wizard was wacky. His spells seemed tacky.

Name _____ Date _____

Agree to Agree

Subjects and verbs must agree. Singular verbs go with singular subjects. Here's an example: "The slipper is glass." Likewise, plural verbs go with plural subjects: "Mermaids are merry." For the exercise below, draw lines to match the subjects with the appropriate verbs.

1. The fox   are clever.

The foxes   is clever.

2. Little Red Riding Hood   walks through the woods.

Hansel and Gretel   walk through the woods.

3. The shoemaker   live in a tiny cottage.

The elves   lives in a tiny cottage.

4. The first Billy Goat Gruff   cross the bridge.

Three Billy Goats Gruff   crosses the bridge

5. Magic beans   fetch a good price at the market.

A magic carpet   fetches a good price at the market.

6. Somebody   need to feed the king's pet tiger.

Others   needs to feed the king's pet tiger.

7. The gingerbread house   is trimmed with gumdrops.

The gingerbread houses   are trimmed with gumdrops.

8. The magic mirror   answer the queen's questions.

The magic mirrors   answers the queen's questions.

Learning Extension: Imagine a pair of mixed-up characters called the Singular Twins. There are two of them, of course, but they use only singular verbs. Here's an example: "We is twins. We likes to ride bikes." Write a Singular Twins tale. By breaking the rules of grammar, you will get a good feel for subject-verb agreement. Then exchange your story with a classmate, and make the verbs match the subjects.

ADJECTIVES

Adjectives add spice. They're used to pump up otherwise dull, dreary sentences. They can be as simple as colors (*red* or *blue*) or sizes (*large* or *small*). Other examples of adjectives include *bold* and *bright*, *energetic* and *enigmatic*, *funny* and *fantastic*. Adjectives modify nouns (the *enormous, green* giant). Predicate adjectives can modify nouns or pronouns. (The giant is *enormous*. He is also *green*.) Adjectives make it possible to turn a grin into a *shy* grin or *toothy* grin.

Adjectives answer the questions "What kind?" (*green* giant, *friendly* giant), "How many?" (*five* giants, *many* giants), and "Which one?" (*that* giant, *this* giant). Of course, there are different types of adjectives, including:

✦ common adjectives, such as *cheerful* or *red*.

✦ proper adjectives, which are formed from proper nouns. Examples include *Italian* and *Victorian*.

✦ compound adjectives, which are formed by putting two words together, such as *warm-blooded* or *old-fashioned*.

✦ comparative and superlative adjectives, such as the sequence *good, better,* and *best. Good* is a plain old adjective. *Better* is the comparative form, and *best* is the superlative.

Here's a great way to get started with teaching adjectives. Walk around your classroom, pointing out various objects and modifying them with adjectives. For example, you might point to the clock and say, "That's an *elegant* clock." As you proceed, you might want to put emphasis on the adjectives: "That is a *green* plant." See if students can figure out what you're up to. Then encourage them to follow your lead. Have students take turns pointing out classroom objects and describing them using their own adjective choices.

Reproducibles to Reinforce Learning

A good introduction to adjectives is *The Three Microscopic Pigs* (page 15). *On Board With Adjectives* (page 16) helps students get a handle on the three questions adjectives answer. To help teach comparative and superlative adjectives, pass out *Fair, Fairer, and Fairest* (page 17).

The Three Microscopic Pigs

Rewrite "The Three Little Pigs," using words from the adjective box or your own adjectives. Feel free to be very silly. Don't forget to put a new adjective in the title.

Adjective Box

adorable	crisp	green	old	sly	thin
angry	elegant	humongous	pink	sneaky	tough
brilliant	fluffy	messy	polka-dotted	sturdy	wacky
bubbly	funny	musty	red	sweet	weak
crabby	giant	neat	scary	teeny	wild

The Three _____ **Pigs**

Once upon a time, there were three _____ pigs.

The first _____ pig was _____.

He built a _____ house out of _____

straw. The _____ wolf huffed and puffed and blew it down.

The second _____ pig was _____.

He built a _____ house out of _____

sticks. The wolf blew his house down, too.

But the third pig was _____. He built a _____

house out of _____ bricks. It had a _____

door made out of _____ steel. The _____

wolf huffed. He puffed. He couldn't blow the house down.

The three little pigs lived happily ever after in the _____

house. They were never bothered again by the _____ wolf.

Learning Extension: Create your own fill-in-the-blank fairy tale. Leave a blank anywhere that an adjective goes. Have a classmate fill in the blanks.

Name _____   Date _____

On Board With Adjectives

Underline the adjectives in the story below.

One fine day, the Big Bad Wolf, Sleeping Beauty, and Pinocchio decided to go skateboarding together. These friends loved sports. Pinocchio had five skateboards, but this skateboard was his favorite one. Sleeping Beauty had a cool skateboard, too. It was covered with pink decals. The wolf brought the coolest skateboard of all. It had eight wheels and was covered in white carpet. It looked kind of like a fluffy rabbit.

The three friends did several tricks on their skateboards. First, Pinocchio did a flip, landed on his long nose, and spun around for four minutes. That trick amazed the wolf and Sleeping Beauty. Next, the wolf kicked his skateboard into the air, caught it in his huge mouth, and gobbled it down. Sleeping Beauty did the strangest trick of all. While skateboarding, she fell asleep. Fortunately, she landed in some soft grass. She was fine and just lay there in a deep slumber.

Learning Extension: Read the above passage again. Find two adjectives that answer each kind of question:

What kind? *fine* day _____   _____

How many? *five* skateboards _____   _____

Which one or ones? *these* friends _____   _____

     No Boring Practice, Please! Funny Fairy Tale Grammar Scholastic Teaching Resources

Name _____   Date _____

Fair, Fairer, and Fairest

The eight sequences below contain a common adjective and the comparative and superlative forms of that adjective. Use the first sequence as an example, and then fill in the blanks for the others.

1. Tom Thumb is <u>small</u>.
The Frog Prince is <u>smaller</u>.
The pea under the mattress is <u>smallest</u>.

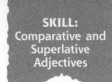

2. Cinderella has <u>long</u> hair. Snow White has _____ hair. Rapunzel has the _____ hair.

3. Learning a magic spell is <u>good</u>. Getting rescued from a dragon is <u>better</u>. Living happily ever after is _____.

4. Jack is <u>tall</u>. The giant is _____. The beanstalk is _____.

5. The three bears had _____ luck. The three little pigs had <u>worse</u> luck. Hansel and Gretel had the _____ luck.

6. Cinderella's stepsisters are <u>mean</u>. Ogres are _____. The Big Bad Wolf is _____.

7. The first pig was <u>smart</u>. The second pig was _____. The third pig was _____.

8. The Enchanted Forest was _____. The castle on the cliff was <u>scarier</u>. The dungeon in the castle was _____.

Learning Extension: Write a fairy tale featuring comparative and superlative adjectives. For example, you could have three brothers who are *wise, wiser,* and *wisest.* They could ride three stallions that are *fast, faster,* and *fastest.*

No Boring Practice, Please! Funny Fairy Tale Grammar Scholastic Teaching Resources

17

ADVERBS

As their name suggests, adverbs modify verbs. They explain various actions, providing information about when, where, how, or to what extent something happened. Here are some examples:

✦ "The queen will now see you." In this case, *now* is an adverb modifying the verb *see*. It answers the question: When will the queen see you?

✦ "The queen sits back on her throne." In this case, *back* is the adverb, and *sits* is the verb. The adverb answers the question: Where does the queen sit?

✦ "The queen sits regally on her throne." *Sits* is the verb again, but this time it's modified by the adverb *regally*. The adverb answers the question: How does the queen sit?

Adverbs can also modify adjectives and other adverbs:

✦ "Cinderella was so happy to meet her fairy godmother." (*So* modifies the adjective *happy* and tells to what extent she was happy.)

✦ "After the ball, Cinderella ran home very quickly." (*Very* modifies the adverb *quickly* and tells to what extent she ran quickly.)

To get students started thinking about this part of speech, write some sentences containing adverbs on the board. Ask questions about when, where, or how the action took place. Then provide a few examples that demonstrate how adverbs can show to what extent something is done. This will help get your class focused on adverbs. Or, put another way, this will *quickly* help your class get *intensely* focused on adverbs.

Reproducibles to Reinforce Learning

Fairy Tale Crimes (page 19) introduces students to the when, where, and how of adverbs. *How Did Chicken Little Cross the Superhighway?* (page 20) and *Goofily Ever After* (page 21) will help students get better acquainted with a vast and helpful family of adverbs, those ending in -*ly*.

SKILL:
Adverbs

Fairy Tale Crimes

Adverbs answer the questions *When? Where? How?* and *To what extent?* Imagine that you were a witness to the following fairy tale crimes. Officer Tad Pole will ask you questions about when, where, how, and to what extent various events happened. Answer using only adverbs.

1. A cow jumped over the moon recently. This caused everyone to look up. That was just the distraction the dish needed. He quickly ran away with the spoon.

Officer Tad Pole's Questions:

When did you say that this cow jumped over the moon? _____ recently _____

I see. Where did everyone look? _____

Uh-huh. How did the dish run? _____

2. Goldilocks broke into the Three Bears' house yesterday. She fit snugly in Baby Bear's chair. But then she completely broke it.

Officer Tad Pole's Questions:

When exactly did Goldilocks break into the bears' home? _____

Interesting. Now, how did she fit in Baby Bear's chair? _____

I understand she damaged Baby Bear's chair. How badly was it broken?

_____

Learning Extension: Write some short stories, two or three sentences long. Make sure to use adverbs that explain when, where, how, and to what extent.

No Boring Practice, Please! Funny Fairy Tale Grammar Scholastic Teaching Resources

19

Name _____   Date _____

How Did Chicken Little Cross the Superhighway?

Adverbs that describe how something happens are among the most common and useful. Question: How did Chicken Little cross the superhighway? Answer: *quickly, slowly, timidly.* Those are just three possible answers. There are a huge number of adverbs that end in -*ly.* Try to think of eight adverbs that can be used in the following sentence. If you do, Chicken Little will safely cross the superhighway.

Chicken Little walked _____quickly_____ across the superhighway.

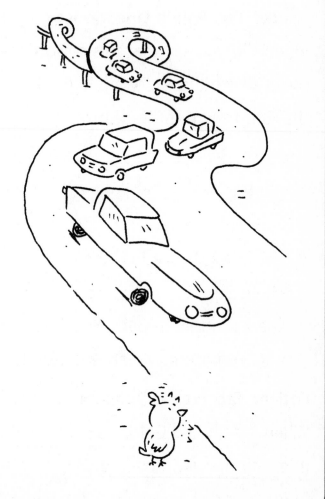

1. _____

2. _____

3. _____

4. _____

5. _____

6. _____

7. _____

8. _____

Learning Extension: Adverbs such as *swiftly* and *boldly* are great for describing action. Write a sports fairy tale featuring a favorite character playing soccer or driving a race car. Use lots of adverbs.

No Boring Practice, Please! Funny Fairy Tale Grammar Scholastic Teaching Resources

Goofily Ever After

Fill in the blanks to create adverbs and complete the following totally fractured tale.

Prince Charming walked _____ly down the street.

He ran into the Three Little Pigs, who were _____ly building

a house. Nearby, the Big Bad Wolf was _____ly popping

a breath mint in his mouth.

The prince also noticed that Jack was _____ly climbing

a beanstalk. He also saw Goldilocks nearby, _____ly

eating a bowl of porridge.

_____ly, a little bird landed on the prince's

shoulder. "The sky is falling down!" he chirped.

The prince _____ly looked up. But it wasn't true.

The sky wasn't falling down. Hansel and Gretel were _____ly

flying a stunt plane and _____ly tossing bread crumbs.

The prince, the pigs, the wolf, Jack,

Goldilocks, and the little bird raced

about, _____ly

catching the crumbs in their mouths. They

all lived _____ly ever after.

Learning Extension: Do the same exercise again, but this time use a totally different set of
adverbs. Don't worry—the supply is endless!

No Boring Practice, Please! Funny Fairy Tale Grammar Scholastic Teaching Resources

21

PRONOUNS

Pronouns can take the place of nouns. *They* make *it* possible to write more clearly and succinctly. Common pronouns include *he*, *she*, *them*, *you*, and *us*. There's a classic Chinese fairy tale about a character named Tikki Tikki Tembo No Sarimbo Hari Kari Bushkie Perry Pem Do Hai Kai Pom Pom Nikki No Meeno Dom Barako. What a mouthful! The character falls down a well and by the time the news gets passed along, with various people using his very long name, it's too late. It would have been better if they had used pronouns, in a sentence such as "Help, he fell down a well!"

Here's an idea to get your class thinking about pronouns. Select a student, and say something like: "Jenny is Jenny's name. Jenny is carrying the blue backpack that belongs to Jenny." It probably won't take long before your students sense that something is up, grammarwise. See if they can figure out the problem. Then explain that you're not using pronouns, and describe what pronouns are and how they are used.

There are a huge number of different pronouns, and one of the challenges is making sure to follow the rules of agreement. These rules can get pretty complicated and specialized. But here are a couple that your students may find particularly useful.

Rule #1: Always make sure that pronouns show gender agreement. If the name *Jenny* is replaced with a pronoun, for example, it needs to be a feminine pronoun such as *she* or *her*.

Rule #2: Always make sure that pronouns agree in number. That is, singular nouns should be replaced by singular pronouns. "Goldilocks ate the porridge" becomes "She ate it." Plural nouns are replaced by plural pronouns. "The three bears were furious" becomes "They were furious."

Reproducibles to Reinforce Learning

Pronouns to the Rescue! (page 23) gives students a feel for how useful pronouns are. *Clued In* (page 24) provides further pronoun practice, while *Cross the Bridge* (page 25) helps students with the rules of pronoun agreement.

Pronouns to the Rescue!

The sentences below are needlessly wordy. Send in the pronouns! Cross out some of the repetitive proper nouns or common nouns. Write pronouns in their place.

1. Grumpy, Sleepy, Happy, Dopey, Bashful, Sneezy, and Doc were seven friends. Although Grumpy, Sleepy, Happy, Dopey, Bashful, Sneezy, and Doc were very different from one another, Grumpy, Sleepy, Happy, Dopey, Bashful, Sneezy, and Doc got along just fine.

2. King Midas had the golden touch. King Midas touched a bike, T-shirt, peach, wristwatch, and pair of scissors. King Midas turned the bike, T-shirt, peach, wristwatch, and pair of scissors to gold.

3. The evil queen owned a magic mirror. The evil queen would ask the magic mirror, "Mirror, Mirror, on the wall, who's the fairest of them all?" The magic mirror would answer the evil queen, and then the evil queen would ask the magic mirror more questions.

Learning Extension: Now try writing a fairy tale or story of your own—without using any pronouns. As you'll quickly see, it's a lot of words and a lot of work, and there's plenty of room for confusion. Then switch papers with a classmate and replace some of the nouns with pronouns.

No Boring Practice, Please! Funny Fairy Tale Grammar Scholastic Teaching Resources

23

Name _____   Date _____

Clued In

Below are 10 clues featuring pronouns such as *he*, *she*, and *they*. Match the clues with the letters for the correct fairy tale characters. Then circle all the pronouns.

CLUES

1. _____ He has a wooden nose.

2. _____ She has very long hair.

3. _____ It lays golden eggs.

4. _____ Anything he touches turns to gold.

5. _____ They are friends who like cheese.

6. _____ They are enemies.

7. _____ She gives the bears a fright.

8. _____ He runs as fast as he can.

9. _____ When he plays music, people follow him.

10. _____ When they play music, it scares off robbers.

"I am turning it all to gold."

CHARACTERS

A. King Midas

B. The Gingerbread Man

C. The Pied Piper

D. Rapunzel

E. Jack and the Giant

F. The Goose

G. The Bremen Town Musicians

H. Pinocchio

I. Country Mouse and City Mouse

J. Goldilocks

Learning Extension: Think of five clues featuring pronouns. For example: *They* were the first to fly an airplane. Answer: the Wright brothers. Exchange your clues with classmates, and guess the answers.

No Boring Practice, Please! Funny Fairy Tale Grammar Scholastic Teaching Resources

Name _____   Date _____

Cross the Bridge

Just as subjects and verbs must agree, there are also rules of agreement for pronouns.
For example, "Rapunzel was tired so he took a nap" would be wrong. Rapunzel is female, so
the sentence requires an appropriate pronoun—*she*. In the exercise below, circle the correct
pronoun, so that the billy goats can cross the bridge.

1. There are three Billy Goats Gruff, and _____ want to cross a bridge.

(them, he, they)

2. The bridge is long, and underneath _____ lives a mean troll.

(themselves, it, its)

3. The troll tries to make the trip across the bridge difficult for _____.

(they, it, them)

4. But the eldest billy goat chases _____ away.

(his, him, them)

5. Finally, the three goats cross and gorge _____ on grass.

(themselves, himself, itself)

Learning Extension: Follow the model above to write a short story that gives choices of
pronouns. Then switch papers with a partner, and circle the correct pronouns.

No Boring Practice, Please! Funny Fairy Tale Grammar Scholastic Teaching Resources

25

PREPOSITIONS

Here's an old favorite that may take you back to your grammar school days: A preposition is anywhere that a squirrel can be in relation to a log. Pretty simple. After all, a squirrel can be *on, under, above, against, near,* or *around* a log. Of course, there are certain prepositions such as *before* and *after* that don't seem to make sense at first. How can a squirrel be after a log? Here's one possible answer: *Squirrel* comes after *log* in the alphabet. Not a bad rule!

One way to get students thinking about prepositions is to take an object such as a pen or an eraser and set it in various places around the room. You could put it on your desk, under your desk, or even hold it above your head. Ask students where the object is. Point out the prepositions in their responses.

Prepositions appear in prepositional phrases. These phrases include the preposition and the object of the preposition, which is a noun or pronoun. Sometimes the phrase will include words that modify the object of the preposition as well. Sometimes there will be more than one object of the preposition. Here are some examples. (*P.* stands for preposition; *O.P.* stands for object of the preposition.)

We are going *to the lighthouse*.
             P   O.P.

We are going *to the tall lighthouse*.
             P.   O.P.

The present is *for Tanya and Michelle*.
          P. O.P   O.P.

The present is *for them*.
          P. O.P.

Reproducibles to Reinforce Learning

Once Upon a Time... (page 27) is a good exercise to introduce students to prepositions. *Pin the Preposition on the Ogre* (page 28) and *Crossword Puzzle* (page 29) serve to reinforce learning about this vital part of grammar. If students need help with the puzzle, provide the answers in a word bank.

Name _____   Date _____

Once Upon a Time . . .

Read the following retelling of "The Princess and the Pea." The first preposition is underlined.
Find and underline 18 others.

Once <u>upon</u> a time, there was a very sleepy princess. She sluggishly
shuffled into the royal chambers and lay on her huge, princess-sized bed. But
even though she felt a huge weariness within her, she could not fall asleep.
There seemed to be something under the mattress, pressing against her side.

The princess shifted onto her other side. Now the thing underneath
her felt even larger, poking into her side. Whatever was beneath her
mattress must be enormous, she thought.

This was unacceptable to the
princess. She stood by her bed scratching
behind her head. Then she lifted the
mattress and looked under it. There she
spotted a teeny, tiny pea. Apparently,
that was all that stood between the
princess and a good night's sleep.
She threw the pea out the royal window
and into the royal courtyard. Then she
climbed upon her bed once again. The
princess slept happily through the night.

Learning Extension: When the princess is awake, she enjoys watching the royal juggler.
Describe some of his tricks, using as many prepositions as possible, such as *above*, *under*,
over, and *between*.

Name _____ Date _____

Pin the Preposition on the Ogre

Here are a few prepositions: *above, below, beside, near,* and *underneath.* Write each preposition in the appropriate place in relation to the ogre. The first one has been done for you. The word *on* has been placed *on* the ogre.

Now use these prepositions in five sentences about the ogre.

Example: The ogre plants stinkweed *in* his garden.

1. against _____

2. over _____

3. from _____

4. beyond _____

5. between _____

Learning Extension: Think of five more prepositions. Now write five more sentences featuring the ogre or another fairy tale character.

Crossword Puzzle

Fill in the crossword puzzle, using the correct prepositions. The first one has been done for you.

Across

1. The royal dessert was served __after__ the royal feast.

2. The prince stood _____ the tower waiting for Rapunzel.

3. The feast was held _____ the castle.

Down

1. The giant towered _____ Jack.

3. Cinderella's foot fit _____ the glass slipper.

4. Jack and Jill went _____ the hill.

| | A | F | T | E | R |

Learning Extension: To create an acrostic, think of words that begin with the letters in a word. For example, here's a preposition acrostic for *wolf*. See how many prepositions you can think of that start with the letters in the name *Aladdin*.

With
Over
Like
From

No Boring Practice, Please! Funny Fairy Tale Grammar Scholastic Teaching Resources

29

CONJUNCTIONS

Reproducibles to Reinforce Learning

Seven Little Magic Words (page 31) and *Gwen and Len* (page 32) teach students about coordinating conjunctions. *Power Pairs* (page 33) will familiarize them with the five pairs of correlative conjunctions.

Conjunctions perform a very important function. They link words or phrases together. In fact, the previous two sentences could benefit from another conjunction. Conjunctions perform a very important function because they link words or phrases together. Here, the added conjunction is *because*. There are actually three different kinds of conjunctions: coordinating conjunctions, correlative conjunctions, and subordinating conjunctions. The activities in this section focus on the first two. Subordinating conjunctions are often taught in upper grades, when students study phrases and clauses in more depth.

✦ *Coordinating conjunctions* These are little words that link together words or phrases. There are only seven coordinating conjunctions in the English language: *and, but, for, nor, or, so,* and *yet.*

✦ *Correlative conjunctions* These are pairs of words that once again serve to connect phrases and create complete sentences. There are only five of these: *both/and, either/or, neither/nor, not only/but also,* and *whether/or.* Here's an example of correlative conjunctions used in a sentence: "Neither the tortoise nor the hare could outrace the snail."

✦ *Subordinating conjunctions* These conjunctions often begin a clause (such as "When winter comes . . .") to link the clause to the rest of the sentence (". . . we will go skiing"). Unlike the other two conjunction forms, there are a huge number of subordinating conjunctions, including *because, where, when, though,* and *before.* Some of these words can also be used as prepositions, which makes this concept difficult for younger students.

Probably the best way to introduce conjunctions to students is to say aloud some sentences featuring them. Pause for a long beat before each conjunction and put emphasis on it when you say it. For example: "We wanted to play outside during recess . . . *but* it's raining." Then write these sentences on the board and discuss the function of the conjunctions.

Seven Little Magic Words

Coordinating conjunctions link words or groups of words together. There are only seven of these words: *and, but, for, nor, or, so,* and *yet.* Pick the best conjunction to complete the following sentences.

1. The witch was clever, _____ Hansel and Gretel outsmarted her.
A) nor   **B)** or   **C)** but   **D)** for

2. Are you more like the Country Mouse _____ the City Mouse?
A) and   **B)** yet   **C)** so   **D)** or

3. The fox jumped higher and higher, _____ he still couldn't reach the grapes.
A) yet   **B)** or   **C)** so   **D)** nor

4. "Rumpelstiltskin" _____ "Rapunzel" are both fairy tales told by the Brothers Grimm.
A) but   **B)** and   **C)** nor   **D)** for

5. Little Red Riding Hood is in a rush, _____ she must get to her grandmother's house.
A) but   **B)** yet   **C)** for   **D)** or

6. Johnny Appleseed planted trees, _____ now everyone has apples.
A) so   **B)** nor   **C)** or   **D)** yet

7. The glass slipper did not fit the first stepsister who tried it on, _____ did it fit the second stepsister.
A) so   **B)** but   **C)** nor   **D)** and

Learning Extension: Create a sausage-link sentence. See how many of these conjunctions you can use in one silly sentence. For example: "Cinderella *and* Sleeping Beauty were friends, *yet* they had their differences, *for* one was wide awake *but* the other was asleep." Whew! Four conjunctions in that one!

No Boring Practice, Please! Funny Fairy Tale Grammar Scholastic Teaching Resources

31

Name _____   Date _____

Gwen and Len

Remember the seven coordinating conjunctions? Underline them in the story below.

Gwen and Len were walking through the Enchanted Forest. Gwen took one path, but Len took another. Len quickly felt lost, for he didn't see anything he recognized. He did not want to stay on an unfamiliar path, nor did he want to wander farther away from Gwen. He knew he needed to turn around or he might not find his way back. Meanwhile, Gwen was clever, so she returned to the exact spot where the path split. She waited patiently, yet she started to get tired. When Len finally returned, they continued on their way.

Learning Extension: In the story above, did you notice that the seven coordinating conjunctions appear in alphabetical order: *and, but, for, nor, or, so, yet?* Now write a story of your own in which the coordinating conjunctions appear in reverse alphabetical order.

Power Pairs

Correlative conjunctions link sentences together. Only five of these "power pairs" exist. See if you can find the power pairs in the following sentences. Write them in the spaces below. The first one has been done for you.

1. Neither Tom Thumb nor Thumbelina liked wearing oversized T-shirts.
Power pair: _____neither_____/_____nor_____

2. Both King Midas and the emperor were royally silly in their behavior.

Power pair: _____/_____

3. Either Pinocchio had the most amazing life ever or he was stretching the truth a bit.

Power pair: _____/_____

4. The story is all about whether Jack will get the treasures or the Giant will get Jack.

Power pair: _____/_____

5. Tikki Tikki Tembo No Sarimbo Hari Kari Bushkie Perry Pem Do Hai Kai Pom Pom Nikki No Meeno Dom Barako is not only a long name but also a difficult one to remember.

Power pair _____/_____

Learning Extension: Write a brief retelling of a fairy tale that includes all five correlative conjunction power pairs.

No Boring Practice, Please! Funny Fairy Tale Grammar Scholastic Teaching Resources

33

CAPITALIZATION

Capitalization is used to emphasize certain words. By capitalizing certain words, we can show that they are not ordinary words and that there is some reason we are calling attention to them. There are a huge variety of instances in which capitalization is necessary. But here are some of the most common:

+ the first letter of a word that begins a sentence

+ proper names in the real world (Paul Newman) and the fictional world (Paul Bunyan)

+ geographic locations both real (Norway) and imaginary (Narnia)

+ days (Sunday), months (July), and holidays (Labor Day)

+ official names of products

+ adjectives that are formed from proper nouns (Italian food)

+ the pronoun *I*

+ titles such as *Miss, Mr.,* or *Mrs.*

+ official titles such as *Sir* or *General* or *Dame,* as in Sir Isaac Newton

+ greetings in letters, such as *Dear*

+ important words as well as first and last words in titles of magazines, books, albums, movies, songs, and so on. An example is *A House Is a House for Me.* Note that the less important words (*a* and *for*) are not capitalized in this case. Even though the verb *is* is a short word, verbs are considered important words.

To get students thinking about capitalization, try out various sentences on them. Put emphasis on the capitalized words: "Did you go to *Central Park* on *Wednesday*?" Ask students to discuss what is different about the emphasized words.

Reproducibles to Reinforce Learning

The exercise *Troll on Tour* (page 35) introduces students to some of the rules of capitalization. The two exercises that follow, *Puppet Beat* (page 36) and *Dear Ant* (page 37), furnish context for the rules and provide students with additional practice.

Name _____ Date _____

Troll on Tour

Read the passage below. Some words are lowercase that should be capitalized and some are capitalized that should be lowercase. Proofread this passage and correct the capitalization. Use these standard proofreading marks: july 10   a great book

I am tired of living under a Bridge. I have decided to travel and show the

World how interesting I am. I have written a book called *thirty Troll Tips for*

A long, Happy life. I have made a CD called *rock and Roll troll*. I will be

going on a concert tour this Summer to miami, Cleveland, and San diego.

I even have a product called mr. Troll's terrible-Tasting toothpaste. Not only

does it taste gross but it also turns your teeth yellow.

Learning Extension: In a book title such as *The Cat in the Hat*, you may have noticed that only the important words are capitalized. Create five fairy tale book titles, such as *The Big Bad Wolf's Guide to Huffing and Puffing and Blowing Down Houses*. They can be as long as you like, but remember not to capitalize words like *and* or *to*, unless they are the first or last word in the title.

Name _____   Date _____

Puppet Beat

Complete Pinocchio's profile for *Puppet Beat* magazine. Remember to follow capitalization rules.

Puppet Beat Magazine • August 2009
Puppet of the Month

Check out the profile below to learn all about one of the world's coolest wooden dudes, Pinocchio.

My Heroes
Gepetto

_____

Favorite Holidays
National Hug-a-Puppet Day

_____

Favorite Movies
Woodshop 3: The Revenge of the Puppets

_____

Favorite Books

_____

_____

Favorite Stores

_____

_____

Favorite Singers or Bands

_____

_____

Learning Extension: Create a profile for a different fairy tale character. You can dream up other categories that require capitalization, such as favorite songs.

Name _____   Date _____

Dear Ant

Correct this letter from Grasshopper to Ant. Note that Grasshopper has failed to capitalize some words and has used capitalization where he shouldn't have. Use these standard proofreading marks: july 10   a great book

tuesday, november 2, 2008

dear ant:

i am writing you because halloween just happened, which reminded me that thanksgiving is coming soon. This reminded me that I did not gather enough Food over the summer. please Help!

I realize that i goofed off all summer long. While you and mrs. ant worked hard gathering food, I went to see the beetles in concert. I also sneaked away to see the movie *ants attack a picnic Basket*. how could you expect me to ignore this excellent entertainment? I'm just a simple Insect, and I like to have Fun!

I wish I did not have to trouble you with this Letter. I just went to my Cupboard, though, and i have only one treat left. please send me something. Since winter is coming, i would be willing to eat your Ant Food, even though I do not usually enjoy that kind of thing. saY hello to your children and mrs. ant.

sincerely,

grasshopper

Learning Extension: Write another letter from one fairy tale character to another, following the rules of capitalization. Fill your letter with proper names, days, holidays, and movie and song titles, so that you can use as much capitalization as possible.

No Boring Practice, Please! Funny Fairy Tale Grammar Scholastic Teaching Resources

37

SENTENCES

One way to think of sentences is as trains, with words as the individual cars. Of course, the train needs to be just the right size. It won't run right if it's too short or lacks a crucial car such as the engine or caboose. Certainly, it won't run well if it is too long, weighted down with too many words and too many meanings.

To make sure that sentences are organized correctly, there are several especially useful rules:

- ✦ *There must be a subject and predicate.* The subject is a noun or pronoun and the predicate is a verb or verb phrase. Both of these parts of grammar are needed to create a proper sentence.

- ✦ *Avoid fragments.* Fragments are incomplete thoughts that hang in the air. They feel as though they need something more. Here's an example: "When Jack planted the magic beans." Note that this phrase has a subject (*Jack*) and a verb (*planted*). To be a proper sentence, it needs something more, such as "The beanstalk grew when Jack planted the magic beans."

- ✦ *Avoid run-on sentences.* A sentence is a run-on when there is a wealth of information contained within it that is not easy to understand because the sentence keeps going on for such a long time by adding new information that complicates matters. That was quite a run-on! The solution is to break down such sentences into a series of sentences. It makes for clearer communication.

To introduce your class to sentences, write some examples on the board. You might start by writing proper sentences and diagramming them to show the subject and predicate. Then write some fragments and run-ons and discuss why they don't work.

Reproducibles to Reinforce Learning

Draw the Line (page 39) is a simple diagramming exercise that will introduce students to subjects and predicates. *Report Card* (page 40) helps students identify and avoid fragments, while *Fairy Tale Fix-It* (page 41) provides an opportunity to repair a very long run-on sentence.

Name _____   Date _____

Draw the Line

Every proper sentence has both a subject and predicate. The subject is like the star of the sentence. The predicate is the word or phrase that contains a verb and explains the action.

Example: <u>A genie</u> <u>popped out of the lamp.</u>
          subject   predicate

In the sentences below, draw lines to separate subjects and predicates. The first one has been done for you.

1. Sleeping Beauty / grew very tired.

2. Br'er Rabbit hid in the briar patch.

3. You would probably enjoy seeing a movie about Hansel and Gretel.

4. The ball was almost over.

5. Goldilocks quickly ate the porridge.

6. The slow and steady tortoise won the race.

7. The frog on the lily pad begged for a kiss.

8. The second little pig with the house made of sticks was scared of the wolf.

9. These are all great fairy tales.

10. The story ended happily ever after.

Learning Extension: By drawing lines, you separated subjects from predicates. Now use only the subjects in the sentences above and write 10 new sentences with different predicates.

Name _____ Date _____

Report Card

Fill out the report card below. If it's a sentence, write an A in the space provided. But if it's a fragment, write an F. Here's a tip: A sentence must contain both a subject and a verb, and it must express a complete thought. If it doesn't, it's a fragment.

Little Red Riding Hood
The Faraway Land School for Girls

1. Little Red Riding Hood is excellent at math. _____

2. Because she has fallen behind in her reading homework. _____

3. Working on a group project in social studies class. _____

4. She wrote a first-rate report on wolves for science class. _____

5. The poem she wrote for her grandma was excellent. _____

6. In gym class, which was terrific. _____

7. Which shows improvement. _____

8. She gets along well with others. _____

9. Prefers reading nonfiction. _____

10. When she arrives at school. _____

Learning Extension: Now help Little Red Riding Hood get straight A's! Fix the sentence fragments above by turning them into proper sentences.

No Boring Practice, Please! Funny Fairy Tale Grammar Scholastic Teaching Resources

Name _____   Date _____

Fairy Tale Fix-It

Pretend you work for a company called Fairy Tale Fix-It. You have several tools in your tool kit, including periods and capitalization. You may also delete words (such as *and*) and add words to smooth things out. Use your tools to break the extra-long sentence below into a set of manageable sentences.

Chicken Little was out walking when an acorn plunked her on the head she thought the sky was falling, so she decided to go tell the king along the way, she ran into Henny Penny she told Henny Penny that the sky was falling they

Fairly Tale Fix-it Call ___

went off together to tell the king on the way, they ran into Cocky Locky and told him the news he agreed that it was terrible, and he joined them the three then set off to find the king they ran into Foxy Woxy and told him about what had happened the fox didn't believe it he was simply annoyed he told them all to stop talking so fast because it was making his head hurt.

Learning Extension: Try your hand at a run-on fairy tale. Then get out your fix-it kit and repair it with periods and capitalization in the proper places.

SENTENCE STOPPERS

Reproducibles to Reinforce Learning

To get the hang of sentence stoppers, students can read *Goldilocks Alison McStibblestubby* (page 43) and select the proper punctuation end marks. *Mystery Guest* (page 44) helps introduce students to sentence stoppers, while *Triple Sentences* (page 45) is an effective exercise to explore how a sentence's meaning can be transformed by choosing from among various punctuation marks.

Sentences must be stopped or there is a risk that they could go on and on and on. Fortunately, there are three versatile sentence stoppers to choose from. They keep written language orderly and make it more expressive.

✦ *Periods* These punctuation marks are small, but they play a huge grammatical role. They are the most common sentence stoppers. Sentences both short and long can be brought to a halt with a simple period.

✦ *Question marks* If a sentence takes the form of a question, it should end with a question mark. For example: "What will happen if I climb this beanstalk?"

✦ *Exclamation points* They make it possible to express excitement, shock, or urgency. For example: "Oh no! There's a giant up here!"

To get students started thinking about sentence stoppers, write a sentence on the board. It can be something simple, like "This is fun." End it first with a period, then erase the period and write a question mark. Then replace the question mark with an exclamation point. Read each version aloud. Chances are, your students will notice the changes in the inflection of your voice. After all, sentence stoppers alone can make the same sentence sound different and have a different meaning: "This is fun. This is fun? This is fun!"

Name _____   Date _____

Goldilocks Alison McStibblestubby

As you read the tale below, fill in the correct sentence stoppers: periods, question marks, and exclamation points.

STORYLAND CONFIDENTIAL

Who is Goldilocks___ Most of us only know her as a young girl who sneaked into the home of three bears___ But there is so much more to the Goldilocks story___ For example, did you know that her full name is Goldilocks Alison McStibblestubby___ Did you know that she dyes her hair__ Can you believe those famous golden locks are actually brown___

But wait, there's more___ Turns out, she is close friends with the Boy Who Cried Wolf___ Can you believe it___ The two of them like to get together and shout, "Wolf___" Our investigation revealed that her other pals include the Wicked Witch of the East, the Wicked Witch of the West, and several evil ogres___ That's a tough crowd___

Of course, everyone fell for Goldilocks's story about wandering in the woods and ending up in the bears' home____ Do you think that's the first time she's done this kind of thing___ Our Ms. McStibblestubby has a long history of entering the homes of fairy tale characters___ Shame on you, Goldilocks Alison McStibblestubby___

Learning Extension: Write your own Storyland Confidential, exposing the truth about a well-known fairy tale character. Along with periods, make sure to use plenty of question marks and exclamation points.

Name _____   Date _____

Mystery Guest

For each of the 10 sentences, circle the letter of the correct stopper—a period, question mark, or exclamation point. Then unscramble the 10 letters to discover the mystery guest.

1. The third little pig's house was made of brick___   A) .   B) ?   C) !

2. Who is wiser, the grasshopper or the ant___   K) .   L) ?   M) !

3. The shoemaker got help from some friendly elves___   E) .   F) ?   G) !

4. Who's afraid of the Big Bad Wolf___   H) .   I) ?   J) !

5. The tortoise has won. This is incredible___   A) .   B) ?   C) !

6. How do you make stone soup___   Q) .   R) ?   S) !

7. The villain is horrible___   B) .   C) ?   D) !

8. The lion was smart to let the mouse go free___   L) .   M) ?   N) !

9. Did Beauty and the Beast live happily ever after___   D) .   E) ?   F) !

10. Chicken Little shouted, "The sky is falling___"   L) .   M) ?   N) !

Mystery Guest

___ ___ ___ ___ ___ ___ ___ ___ ___ ___

Learning Extension: Here is a set of nine sentence stoppers: . . . ? ? ? ! ! ! Now, write a few sentences, or even a very short story, using only this set of nine.

Triple Sentences

The same sentence can have different meanings, based on whether it ends with a period, question mark, or exclamation point. See if you can write the same sentence with each kind of sentence stopper. An example is provided.

●

period

1. This is a fun exercise.

2. _____

3. _____

?

question mark

1. This is a fun exercise?

2. _____

3. _____

!

exclamation point

1. This is a fun exercise!

2. _____

3. _____

Learning Extension: Write a fractured fairy tale that features several periods, question marks, and exclamation points.

COMMAS

Commas create little breaks within sentences, making it possible to separate words and ideas. They play a vital role in clear written communication. As a first step to teaching commas, write the following on the board: "John Henry and Tina got on the bus, followed by Betty Lou and Sam." Ask students how many people got on the bus—four or six? Only the proper use of commas can make that clear. Commas are a popular piece of punctuation, but here are three especially helpful ways in which they are used:

✦ *Commas are used to separate items in a sequence.*
For example, if six people got on the bus, the proper punctuation would be: "John, Henry, and Tina got on the bus, followed by Betty, Lou, and Sam." By leaving out some of these commas, the author can indicate that John Henry is one person and Betty Lou is another.

✦ *Commas are used to insert information into a sentence.*
Here's an example: "Jack, who was a very curious boy, climbed the beanstalk."

✦ *Commas are used to set off direct quotations in various ways.*
Here's the same quotation cast three different ways:
The Big Bad Wolf said, "I'll huff and I'll puff and I'll blow your house down."

"I'll huff and I'll puff," said the Big Bad Wolf, "and I'll blow your house down."

"I'll huff and I'll puff and I'll blow your house down," said the Big Bad Wolf.

Name _____   Date _____

Have a Ball!

The annual ball is taking place at the Enchanted Castle, but someone forgot to proofread the invitations. Add commas wherever they are needed.

You're Invited

Date
February 1 2010

Place
The Enchanted Castle
9999 Never-Ending Lane
Enchanted Forest New Jersey

Guest List
The presence of the following honored guests is requested:
Sleeping Beauty Pinocchio Goldilocks the Big Bad Wolf Rapunzel Rumpelstiltskin and Tom Thumb.

Dining
We shall dine on fine fare:
salad of watercress dandelion and fennel root
purée of parsnips peas and prunes
roasted deer pheasant and partridge
gooseberry tart boysenberry sherbet and huckleberry custard

Directions to the Castle
Take the Royal Turnpike until you reach Exit 9999. Turn right at the stop sign left at the giant oak tree and right at the waterfall. Continue driving for 197 miles. Take a left onto Never-Ending Lane a right at the mailbox and a left over the drawbridge.

Learning Extension: Create a fairy tale recipe. It could be instructions for baking a gingerbread man. You could also list the ingredients for casting a spell to put a princess to sleep. Check your placement of commas.

No Boring Practice, Please! Funny Fairy Tale Grammar Scholastic Teaching Resources

47

Name _____   Date _____

Ye Old Rumor Mill

Below is an imaginary gossip column about various fairy tale characters. Fill in the blanks with additional information about the characters—and don't forget to use commas. The first two items of gossip serve as examples.

LA-LA LAND GAZETTE GOSSIP COLUMN

Cinderella, wearing very stylish glass slippers, was spotted dining with a dashing prince.

The princess, who was kept awake by a pesky pea, has purchased a brand-new waterbed.

1. The Three Little Pigs _____

are shopping for a larger house in which they can all live together.

2. Hansel and Gretel _____

will host a new cooking show on television this fall.

3. Rapunzel _____

has opened a very popular hair salon.

4. The Big Bad Wolf _____

is appearing in a toothpaste commercial.

5. The cow _____ jumped over the moon.

6. The dish _____

ran away with the spoon.

Learning Extension: Now, try your hand at a fairy tale news story. Use commas to insert information into various sentences. This example will help you get started:

"The Gingerbread Man, who is very fast, was seen leaving the bakery. The giant, who has enormous feet, tried to block his way."

Name _____   Date _____

Goldilocks and the Commas

This retelling of the classic fairy tale features plenty of quotations. Fill in the missing commas.

Goldilocks and the Three Bears

A little girl named Goldilocks was gathering flowers in the woods. She spotted a cottage and sneaked inside. She ate three bowls of porridge, sat in three different chairs, and tried out three different beds. She fell asleep in the last one. Presently, the three bears who lived in the cottage returned home.

"Someone has been eating my porridge," said Papa Bear.

"It appears," said Mama Bear, "that someone tasted mine as well."

Baby Bear shrieked, "Someone snarfed down my whole bowl!"

"Someone has been sitting in my chair" said Papa Bear.

"It seems" said Mama Bear "that someone sat in mine as well."

Baby Bear screamed "Oh man! My chair is broken to bits!"

"Someone has been sleeping in my bed" said Papa Bear.

"It is clear" said Mama Bear "that someone slept in mine as well."

Baby Bear howled "Some strange girl is sleeping in my bed!"

"Aaaaaaaagh" shrieked Goldilocks, waking up to the sight of the bears.

She ran out of the house, through the woods, and never returned to the cottage again.

Learning Extension: Create some fairy tale dialogue of your own, perhaps between Little Red Riding Hood and the Big Bad Wolf, or between the tortoise and the hare. Remember to put commas in all the right places.

No Boring Practice, Please! Funny Fairy Tale Grammar Scholastic Teaching Resources

49

QUOTATIONS

Quotation marks form a neat little bracket around the exact words that someone has said. Ever notice that when some people use quotations, they actually raise their fingers in a way that looks kind of like a lobster claw or a lopsided peace sign? Try out some classic quotations on your class. Example: *George Washington said*—then raise your fingers to make quotation marks—*"I cannot tell a lie."* Ask students what special punctuation marks they might see in that sentence if it were written. Then write the sentence to show the quotation marks.

Quotation marks are really pretty simple. Confusion can occur when students try to figure out where to place other punctuation marks in relation to quotation marks. Here are some rules to follow:

✦ *When a quotation is introduced, the comma goes outside the quotation marks.*
The Gingerbread Man said, "You can't catch me."

✦ *To close a quotation, the comma goes inside.*
"You can't catch me," said the Gingerbread Man.

✦ *These rules apply to longer quotations that are split in two.*
"Run as fast as you like," said the Gingerbread Man, "but you can't catch me."

✦ *Provided they're part of the quotation, question marks and exclamation points always go inside.*
The Gingerbread Man said, "You can't catch me!"

✦ *Question marks and exclamation points go outside if they're not part of the quotation.*
Did the Gingerbread Man really say, "You can't catch me"?

✦ *Colons can be used to introduce long quotations or sayings.*
The Gingerbread Man said: "Run as fast as you like. Run all day and night. You can't catch me."

✦ *Quotation marks are also used around the names of short artistic works such as poems or songs.*
One example is "The Ballad of the Gingerbread Man."

Reproducibles to Reinforce Learning

The Tortoise and the Hare (page 51) introduces students to some of the rules for using quotation marks as they add punctuation to a dialogue-filled version of the tale. *Talking Princess Doll* (page 52) helps students get a handle on the placement of quotation marks and other punctuation. *Quotation Match* (page 53) gives students practice with longer quotations that are broken in two.

The Tortoise and the Hare

In the passage below, fix mistakes of various kinds, including missing quotation marks, commas, or other punctuation. Also look for punctuation marks on the wrong side of the quotation marks. Hint: There are 10 mistakes total.

"I am so incredibly fast," bragged Hare

"I'm unbelievably fast" bragged Tortoise.

Hare said, "Don't blink or you might miss me."

Tortoise said "Don't get confused. You could easily mistake my shell for a speeding Indy car!"

Enough of this, boys," said Skunk.

Skunk had been chosen as the referee. He said, "On your mark . . . get set . . . go!

Hare and Tortoise were truly as fast as they claimed. But neither ran in the right direction.

Chipmunk shouted to Hare, You're running in circles!"

Snail warned Tortoise, "You're going the wrong way"!

"This race is terrible" said Otter.

Owl had slept through most of the race. She woke up and asked, Who's winning?"

"Who knows and who cares"? Raccoon replied.

The moral of the story: "Those who boast need help the most."

Learning Extension: Write your own dialogue-filled version of a classic fairy tale. Make sure to follow the proper rules for using quotation marks.

No Boring Practice, Please! Funny Fairy Tale Grammar Scholastic Teaching Resources

51

Name _____   Date _____

Talking Princess Doll

Imagine a toy called a Talking Princess Doll. She can say six different sentences. Fill in the advertisement, using the sentences below. Make sure you properly use quotation marks, commas, and other punctuation.

For just $29.95, you can be the owner of a Talking Princess Doll from Blabco. Pull her string and she actually talks! Batteries not included.

1. At snack time she says _____

2. At bedtime she says _____

3. _____ she says to guests.

4. _____ she says when she wants to play outside.

5. _____ she asks when she spies a dashing amphibian.

6. If you keep pulling her string, she might even scream _____

_____

Sentences

My castle is your castle.
I demand carrots!
I need some royal shut-eye.
Stop pulling my string!
Who is that handsome frog?
I'm going skateboarding.

Learning Extension: Dream up a different fairy tale toy that talks. What would this toy say? Create an advertisement, and make sure to use quotation marks properly.

No Boring Practice, Please! Funny Fairy Tale Grammar Scholastic Teaching Resources

Quotation Match

Sometimes it makes sense to break a longer quotation in two. Match the correct halves of the quotations together. Then find the character who would say each quotation. Write each quotation, using appropriate punctuation. Hint: Use the example as a model.

Column A

I'll huff and I'll puff

I wonder

You must be home by midnight

Since no one helped me

Column B

or your carriage will turn into a pumpkin.

I'll just eat the bread all by myself!

and I'll blow your house down!

who's been eating my porridge.

Example

"I'm so far ahead of Tortoise," said Hare, "that I think I'll take a little nap."

1. _____ said the Big Bad Wolf

_____

2. _____ said the Fairy Godmother

_____

3. _____ said Baby Bear

_____

4. _____ said the Little Red Hen

_____

Learning Extension: Write a few more quotations from fairy tale characters. Break each quotation in two, using the same format as the above sentences.

APOSTROPHES

The apostrophe is a versatile punctuation mark, with some distinctly different uses:

✦ *Apostrophes are used in contractions.* The apostrophe signals that a letter or letters have been removed to join two words together and create a contraction. Here are some examples:

they are = they're
has not = hasn't
I will = I'll
it is = it's
let us = let's

✦ *Apostrophes are used to show possession.* The rules are as follows:
For singular nouns, add an apostrophe and an *s*:
Cinderella's slipper
the *princess's* crown

For plural nouns ending in *s*, you simply add an apostrophe:
the three little *pigs'* problem

For plural nouns not ending in s, add an apostrophe plus an *s*:
the *children's* room

Write an apostrophe on the board and explain to students that this little punctuation mark has several important uses. Then demonstrate how to use apostrophes in contractions and to show possession.

Reproducibles to Reinforce Learning

Crunch Time (page 55) is a fun way to review contractions. *Who's the Owner?* (page 56) introduces the concept of using apostrophes to show possession. *The Emperor's New Tinfoil Ball* (page 57) provides further practice with using apostrophes.

Name _____   Date _____

Crunch Time

Contractions combine two words, removing at least one letter in the process. The apostrophe is used to show that letters have been removed. For example, *do not* becomes *don't*. Now, help Jules the Giant crunch the underlined words below to form contractions.

1. Hi, <u>I am</u> Jules the Giant.

___ ' ___

2. <u>It is</u> nice to eat you . . . oops, I mean meet you.

___ ___ ' ___

3. <u>You are</u> very small and tender . . . uh, I mean friendly.

___ ___ ___ ' ___ ___

4. <u>I will</u> tell you a little bit about myself.

___ ' ___ ___

5. <u>I would</u> love to be a veterinarian, but I am afraid of kittens.

___ ' ___

6. Let me assure you, giants <u>are not</u> good at marbles.

___ ___ ___ ___ ' ___

7. <u>I have</u> got to buy a car with more legroom.

___ ' ___ ___

8. Now, <u>let us</u> be best friends!

___ ___ ___ ' ___

Learning Extension: Try writing some sentences with and without contractions. Example: "I don't believe it. I do not believe it." Either sentence is grammatically correct. But notice that sentences are more casual with contractions and more formal without them.

Name _____ Date _____

Who's the Owner?

Use apostrophes and any letters needed to make the following characters show ownership.
Then write the characters' numbers on the lines beside their possessions.

- For singular nouns, add 's (*Cinderella's slipper, princess's crown*).
- For plural nouns ending in s, add an apostrophe (*students' chairs*).
- For plural nouns not ending in s, add 's (*children's room*).

1. The Three Bears   ____ magic mirror

2. King Midas   ____ picnic basket

3. The Three Little Pigs   ____ instruments

4. The queen   ____ golden hamburger

5. Tortoise   ____ loaf of bread

6. Goldilocks   ____ porridge

7. Rapunzel   ____ houses

8. Bremen Town Musicians   ____ blonde hair

9. Elves   ____ running shoes

10. Little Red Riding Hood ____ bridge

11. Little Red Hen   ____ miniature workshop

12. Troll   ____ extra-long hair

Learning Extension: Make a list of 10 more fairy tale characters and their prize possessions.
Make sure to use apostrophes.

The Emperor's New Tinfoil Ball

Read the fairy tale below. Insert apostrophes wherever they belong. Here's a clue: There are 12 missing apostrophes in the story.

Once upon a time there lived a very greedy emperor. He loved new stuff. He wasnt content with just a few new things. No matter how much he owned, he still couldnt be satisfied.

He didnt use his new stuff at all. Instead, hed simply hide it away in a huge storage room. The emperor had the only key to the room, and it was made of gold.

One day a salesman paid a visit to the emperors palace. "The King of Persias most valuable possession can now be yours," said the salesman, holding up a ball of tinfoil. The salesman turned the ball so that the tinfoils surface sparkled in the light. The emperor admired the glittering orb.

"Its priceless," said the salesman. "Ill trade it for that key." The emperor tore the key off its chain and handed it to him. He snatched the ball from the salesmans hand and rushed off to put it in his special storage room. When he arrived, he realized he didnt have the key anymore. The emperors newest prize was now his only prize: a tinfoil ball.

Learning Extension: In the story above, you may have noticed the difference between *its* and *it's*. As a contraction, *it's* (*it is*) requires an apostrophe. To show possession ("The dog loves *its* bone"), no apostrophe is necessary. Now try writing three sentences featuring *it's* and three featuring *its*.

No Boring Practice, Please! Funny Fairy Tale Grammar Scholastic Teaching Resources

57

HOMOPHONES

The prefix *homo-* means "the same." Homophones are words that sound the same but are spelled differently. Examples include *dear* and *deer*, *hour* and *our*, *flu* and *flew*, and many longer words such as *discussed* and *disgust*.

Homophones are guaranteed to create confusion. So it's important for kids to learn which spellings have which meanings. About the only trick here is memorization—learning the difference between *hear* and *here*, *which* and *witch*, *kernel* and *colonel*. Of course, homophones also make it possible to create some great jokes and puns. Here's an example: "We dressed up our cat for Christmas. We called him Santa Claws."

To introduce students to homophones, try saying aloud some sentences that use pairs of homophones. For example: "*I'll* walk down the *aisle* now and tell you about the *Isle* of Capri." You might also try out some jokes, such as the classic: "What's black and white and *read* all over?" Answer: a newspaper. When kids hear this joke, they will likely interpret *read* for its homophone, *red*. They'll come up with all kinds of answers, providing a perfect opportunity to launch a discussion of homophones.

Reproducibles to Reinforce Learning

There, Their (page 59) is a good way to introduce or review homophones. For further practice, try the crossword puzzle *Homophone Puzzler* (page 60).

Name _____   Date _____

There, Their

Homophones are words that sound the same but have different spellings and meanings.
An example is *buy* and *bye*. The sentences below use the wrong homophones. Write the correct
ones in the blanks. The first one has been done for you.

1. I really love a good <u>ferry</u> tale. _____ fairy _____

2. Have you <u>red</u> "The Emperor's <u>Knew</u> Clothes?" _____ _____

3. He didn't <u>no</u> that he had nothing to <u>where</u>! _____ _____

4. "Little Red Riding Hood" is a good <u>won two</u>. _____ _____

5. She is walking <u>threw</u> the woods and runs <u>write</u> into a big bad wolf.

_____ _____

6. When I'm <u>board</u>, I like <u>too</u> read that one <u>allowed</u>.

_____ _____ _____

7. <u>Hay</u>, what about "The Tortoise and the <u>Hair</u>?" _____ _____

8. You can't <u>beet</u> that <u>tail</u>. _____ _____

9. I <u>wood</u> like to <u>here</u> it every single <u>knight</u>.

_____ _____ _____

10. <u>Witch</u> is your favorite? I think <u>there</u> all terrific!

_____ _____

Learning Extension: Write your own silly sentences with incorrect homophones. Then switch
papers with a classmate and correct them. You might even try to use some triple homophones,
such as *to, too,* and *two* or *aisle, I'll,* and *isle*.

Name _____   Date _____

Homophone Puzzler

Each sentence below has a missing word. This word happens to be a homophone for the underlined word in the same sentence. Fill in the crossword puzzle with the missing words. The first one has been done for you.

Across

1. A ball is <u>thrown</u> and lands on the king's throne _____.

4. The eagle <u>soared</u> high and fetched the _____ from the mountaintop.

6. The <u>two</u> tigers lived _____ close together.

7. The greedy goblin <u>ate</u> _____ bowls of soup.

8. It was a good <u>night</u> for the _____.

Down

2. The knight was <u>hoarse</u> from calling the name of his lost _____.

3. The carriage <u>missed</u> its turnoff and got lost in the _____.

4. The old woman lived in a <u>shoe</u> and had to _____ away flies.

5. No one was sure <u>which</u> _____ had cast the spell.

8. The tailor was <u>new</u> in the town, and nobody _____ him.

Crossword grid across answers:
1 across: **THRONE**

Learning Extension: Write 10 sentences using pairs of homophones—they can be the same homophone pairs in the puzzle or different ones. The sillier your sentences, the better!

No Boring Practice, Please! Funny Fairy Tale Grammar Scholastic Teaching Resources

Answer Key

NOUNS

page 7, Wall of Words
kingdom, tree, ice, sword, tower, lightning, prisoner, moonlight, witch, potion, mirror, apple, castle, forest, cottage

page 8, The Princess and the Spree
Answers will vary. These are possibilities.

Princess Petunia was trying to get to Omaha. She was lost in the Enchanted Forest. She discovered a trail of Dino's Donut crumbs. She followed the trail, and it led to a magic Zowee. She turned on the magic Zowee's radio, and a song by the Pied Piper was playing. She began to clap her hands. After she had clapped three times, the magic Zowee lifted up in the air and few to Omaha. It landed in the parking lot of Fairy Tale Super Store. Perfect! This was exactly where the princess was trying to go in the first place. She went inside, met her friends, and bought some Magic Beans.

page 9, Give Plurals a Whirl
1. Goldilocks and the Three Boars; 2. The Emperor's New Puppies; 3. Snoring Beauties; 4. Three Kitty Cats Gruff; 5. The Teeny Genie and the Three Small Wishes; 6. Pinocchio's Pepperoni Pizza Parties; 7. Snow White and the Seven Snowflakes; 8. The Three Huge Hogs; 9. The Wicked Witches of the West; 10. One Hundred and One Foxes

VERBS

page 11, Lights, Camera, Action!
Answers will vary. These are possibilities.

Cinderella simply had to be home by midnight. She jumped into her hot-rod pumpkin. The horses, which used to be mice, began to sprint. The carriage zipped down the street. It lurched around a corner.

Soon the pumpkin carriage was cruising down the highway. Nobody saw the patch of spilled apple juice until they were about to splash through it. But these were skillful horses. They quickly pranced around the apple juice, and the carriage stayed dry. Soon the carriage was zooming down the road again at full speed.

The horses kept galloping until they reached Cinderella's home. She leapt out and dashed inside. She bolted through the door just before the clock struck midnight.

page 12, Missing Links
1. C) is; 2. D) remain; 3. A) seems; 4. B) felt; 5. C) looks; 6. D) tasted; 7. A) became; 8. D) sounded

page 13, Agree to Agree
1. The fox is clever.
   The foxes are clever.
2. Little Red Riding Hood walks through the woods.
   Hansel and Gretel walk through the woods.
3. The shoemaker lives in a tiny cottage.
   The elves live in a tiny cottage.
4. The first Billy Goat Gruff crosses the bridge.
   Three Billy Goats Gruff cross the bridge.
5. Magic beans fetch a good price at the market.
   A magic carpet fetches a good price at the market.
6. Somebody needs to feed the king's pet tiger.
   Others need to feed the king's pet tiger.
7. The gingerbread house is trimmed with gumdrops.
   The gingerbread houses are trimmed with gumdrops.
8. The magic mirror answers the queen's questions.
   The magic mirrors answer the queen's questions.

ADJECTIVES

page 15, The Three Microscopic Pigs
Answers will vary. These are possibilities.

The Three Tiny Pigs
Once upon a time, there were three tiny pigs. The first wee pig was tired. He built a flimsy house out of yellow straw. The sly wolf huffed and puffed and blew it down. The second itty-bitty pig was clever. He built a fancy house out of many sticks. The wolf blew his house down, too.

But the third pig was brilliant. He built a sturdy house out of red bricks. It had a thick door made out of shiny steel. The crabby wolf huffed. He puffed. He couldn't blow the house down.

The three little pigs lived happily ever after in the brick house. They were never bothered again by the pesky wolf.

page 16, On Board With Adjectives
One fine day, the Big Bad* Wolf, Sleeping* Beauty, and Pinocchio decided to go skateboarding together. These friends loved sports. Pinocchio had five skateboards, but this skateboard was his** favorite one. Sleeping Beauty had a cool skateboard, too. It was covered with pink decals. The wolf brought the coolest skateboard of all. It had eight wheels and was covered in white carpet. It looked kind of like a fluffy rabbit.

The three friends did several tricks on their skateboards. First, Pinocchio did a flip, landed on his long nose, and spun around for four minutes. That trick amazed the wolf and Sleeping Beauty. Next, the wolf kicked his skateboard into the air, caught it in his huge mouth, and gobbled it down. Sleeping Beauty did the strangest trick of all. While skateboarding, she fell asleep. Fortunately, she landed in some soft grass. She was fine and just lay there in a deep slumber.

* *Big, Bad,* and *Sleeping* can be considered adjectives or they can be considered part of the proper nouns *Big Bad Wolf* and *Sleeping Beauty.*

**Please note that some sources identify *his, her,* and *their* as possessive pronouns. Other sources identify them as adjectives. They are underlined as adjectives in the above passage.

page 17, Fair, Fairer, and Fairest
1. answers provided
2. longer, longest
3. best
4. taller, tallest
5. bad, worst
6. meaner, meanest
7. smarter, smartest
8. scary, scariest

ADVERBS

page 19, Fairy Tale Crimes
1. up, quickly
2. yesterday, snugly, completely

page 20, How Did Chicken Little Cross the Superhighway?
Answers will vary. These are possibilities.
1. gracefully
2. loudly
3. cautiously
4. proudly
5. nervously
6. quietly
7. fearfully
8. excitedly

page 21, Goofily Ever After
Answers will vary. These are possibilities.

Prince Charming walked proudly down the street. He ran into the Three Little Pigs, who were carefully building a house. Nearby, the Big Bad Wolf was slyly popping a breath mint in his mouth.

The prince also noticed that Jack was slowly climbing a beanstalk. He also saw Goldilocks nearby, noisily eating a bowl of porridge.

Suddenly, a little bird landed on the prince's shoulder. "The sky is falling down!" he chirped.

The prince fearfully looked up. But it wasn't true. The sky wasn't falling down. Hansel and Gretel were boldly flying a stunt plane and dramatically tossing bread crumbs. The prince, the pigs, the wolf, Jack, Goldilocks, and the little bird raced about, eagerly catching the crumbs in their mouths. They all lived joyfully ever after.

Answer Key

PRONOUNS

page 23, Pronouns to the Rescue!
Answers will vary. These are possibilities.

1. Grumpy, Sleepy, Happy, Dopey, Bashful, Sneezy, and Doc were seven friends. Although <u>they</u> were very different from one another, <u>they</u> got along just fine.
2. King Midas had the golden touch. <u>He</u> touched a bike, T-shirt, peach, wristwatch, and pair of scissors. <u>He</u> turned <u>them</u> to gold.
3. The evil queen owned a magic mirror. <u>She</u> would ask <u>it</u>, "Mirror, Mirror, on the wall, who's the fairest of them all?" The magic mirror would answer <u>her</u>, and then <u>she</u> would ask <u>it</u> more questions.

page 24, Clued In
1. H; <u>He</u> has a wooden nose.
2. D; <u>She</u> has very long hair.
3. F; <u>It</u> lays golden eggs.
4. A; Anything <u>he</u> touches turns to gold.
5. I; <u>They</u> are friends who like cheese.
6. E; <u>They</u> are enemies.
7. J; <u>She</u> gives the bears a fright.
8. B; <u>He</u> runs as fast as <u>he</u> can.
9. C; When <u>he</u> plays music, people follow <u>him</u>.
10. G; When <u>they</u> play music, <u>it</u> scares off robbers.

page 25, Cross the Bridge
1. they
2. it
3. them
4. him
5. themselves

PREPOSITIONS

page 27, Once Upon a Time . . .

Once <u>upon</u> a time, there was a very sleepy princess. She sluggishly shuffled <u>into</u> the royal chambers and lay <u>on</u> her huge, princess-sized bed. But even though she felt a huge weariness <u>within</u> her, she could not fall asleep. There seemed to be something <u>under</u> the mattress, pressing <u>against</u> her side.

The princess shifted <u>onto</u> her other side. Now the thing <u>underneath</u> her felt even larger, poking <u>into</u> her side. Whatever was <u>beneath</u> her mattress must be enormous, she thought.

This was unacceptable <u>to</u> the princess. She stood <u>by</u> her bed scratching <u>behind</u> her head. Then she lifted the mattress and looked <u>under</u> it. There she spotted a teeny, tiny pea. Apparently, that was all that stood <u>between</u> the princess and a good night's sleep. She threw the pea <u>out</u> the royal window and <u>into</u> the royal courtyard. Then she climbed <u>upon</u> her bed once again. The princess slept happily <u>through</u> the night.

page 28, Pin the Preposition on the Ogre
Answers will vary. These are possibilities.

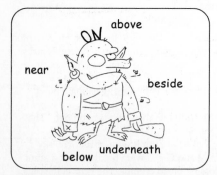

1. The ogre pushed against the door.
2. The ogre jumped over the moat.
3. The ogre received a letter from his cousin.
4. The ogre walked beyond the trees.
5. The ogre sat between his friends.

page 29, Crossword Puzzle

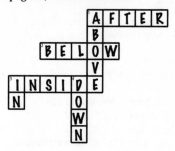

CONJUNCTIONS

page 31, Seven Little Magic Words
1. C) but
2. D) or
3. A) yet
4. B) and
5. C) for
6. A) so
7. C) nor

page 32, Gwen and Len
Gwen <u>and</u> Len were walking through the Enchanted Forest. Gwen took one path, <u>but</u> Len took another. Len quickly felt lost, <u>for</u> he didn't see anything he recognized. He did not want to stay on an unfamiliar path, <u>nor</u> did he want to wander farther away from Gwen. He knew he needed to turn around <u>or</u> he might not find his way back. Meanwhile, Gwen was clever, <u>so</u> she returned to the exact spot where the path split. She waited patiently, <u>yet</u> she started to get tired. When Len finally returned, they continued on their way.

page 33, Power Pairs
1. The answers were provided as a model.
2. both, and
3. either, or
4. whether, or
5. not only, but also

CAPITALIZATION

page 35, Troll on Tour

> I am tired of living under a <u>b</u>ridge. I have decided to travel and show the <u>w</u>orld how interesting I am. I have written a book called *thirty Troll Tips for* <u>A</u> *long, Happy life.* I have made a CD called *rock and Roll troll.* I will be going on a concert tour this <u>s</u>ummer to <u>miami</u>, Cleveland, and <u>san diego</u>. I even have a product called <u>mr.</u> Troll's <u>terrible-Tasting</u> toothpaste. Not only does it taste gross but it also turns your teeth yellow.

page 36, Puppet Beat
Answers will vary. These are possibilities.

My Heroes:	Mother Goose
Favorite Holidays:	Puppeteer Appreciation Day
Favorite Movies:	*The Great Puppet Adventure*
Favorite Books:	*A Marionette's Guide to Everything*
Favorite Stores:	Puppet Emporium
Favorite Singers or Bands:	The Woodwind Quartet

Answer Key

page 37, Dear Ant

tuesday, november 2, 2008

dear ant:

    i am writing you because halloween just happened, which reminded me that thanksgiving is coming soon. This reminded me that I did not gather enough food over the summer. please Help!

    I realize that i goofed off all summer long. While you and mrs. ant worked hard gathering food, I went to see the beetles in concert. I also sneaked away to see the movie ants attack a picnic Basket. how could you expect me to ignore this excellent entertainment? I'm just a simple Insect, and I like to have Fun!

    I wish I did not have to trouble you with this Letter. I just went to my Cupboard, though, and i have only one treat left. please send me something. Since winter is coming, i would be willing to eat your Ant food, even though I do not usually enjoy that kind of thing. say hello to your children and mrs. ant.

    sincerely,
    grasshopper

SENTENCES

page 39, Draw the Line

1. Sleeping Beauty / grew very tired.
2. Br'er Rabbit / hid in the briar patch.
3. You / would probably enjoy seeing a movie about Hansel and Gretel.
4. The ball / was almost over.
5. Goldilocks / quickly ate the porridge.
6. The slow and steady tortoise / won the race.
7. The frog on the lily pad / begged for a kiss.
8. The second little pig with the house made of sticks / was scared of the wolf.
9. These / are all great fairy tales.
10. The story / ended happily ever after.

page 40, Report Card

1. A	5. A	9. F
2. F	6. F	10. F
3. F	7. F	
4. A	8. A	

page 41, Fairy Tale Fix-It

Answers will vary. These are possibilities.

Chicken Little was out walking when an acorn plunked her on the head. She thought the sky was falling, so she decided to go tell the king. Along the way, she ran into Henny Penny. She told Henny Penny that the sky was falling. They went off together to tell the king. On the way, they ran into Cocky Locky and told him the news. He agreed that it was terrible, and he joined them. The three then set off to find the king. They ran into Foxy Woxy and told him about what had happened. The fox didn't believe it. He was simply annoyed. He told them all to stop talking so fast because it was making his head hurt.

SENTENCE STOPPERS

page 43, Goldilocks Alison McStibblestubby

    Who is Goldilocks? Most of us only know her as a young girl who sneaked into the home of three bears. But there is so much more to the Goldilocks story. For example, did you know that her full name is Goldilocks Alison McStibblestubby? Did you know that she dyes her hair? Can you believe those famous golden locks are actually brown?

    But wait, there's more! Turns out, she is close friends with the Boy Who Cried Wolf. Can you believe it? The two of them like to get together and shout, "Wolf!" Our investigation revealed that her other pals include the Wicked Witch of the East, the Wicked Witch of the West, and several evil ogres. That's a tough crowd!

    Of course, everyone fell for Goldilocks's story about wandering in the woods and ending up in the bears' home. Do you think that's the first time she's done this kind of thing? Our Ms. McStibblestubby has a long history of entering the homes of fairy tale characters. Shame on you, Goldilocks Alison McStibblestubby!

page 44, Mystery Guest

1. A	5. C	9. E
2. L	6. R	10. N
3. E	7. D	
4. I	8. L	

Mystery Guest: CINDERELLA

page 45, Triple Sentences

Answers will vary. These are possibilities.

1. The answer was provided as a model.
2. You had a great summer.
   You had a great summer?
   You had a great summer!
3. They are best friends.
   They are best friends?
   They are best friends!

COMMAS

page 47, Have a Ball!

You're Invited

Date
February 1, 2010

Place
The Enchanted Castle
9999 Never-Ending Lane
Enchanted Forest, New Jersey

Guest List
The presence of the following honored guests is requested: Sleeping Beauty, Pinocchio, Goldilocks, the Big Bad Wolf, Rapunzel, Rumpelstiltskin, and Tom Thumb.

Dining
We shall dine on fine fare:
salad of watercress, dandelion, and fennel root
purée of parsnips, peas, and prunes
roasted deer, pheasant, and partridge
gooseberry tart, boysenberry sherbet, and huckleberry custard

Directions to the Castle
Take the Royal Turnpike until you reach Exit 9999. Turn right at the stop sign, left at the giant oak tree, and right at the waterfall. Continue driving for 197 miles. Take a left onto Never-Ending Lane, a right at the mailbox, and a left over the drawbridge.

page 48, Ye Old Rumor Mill

Answers will vary. These are possibilities.

1. The Three Little Pigs, whose homes were damaged by the Big Bad Wolf, are shopping for a larger house in which they can all live together.
2. Hansel and Gretel, who just published their first cookbook, will host a new cooking show on television this fall.
3. Rapunzel, who is known for her extremely long locks, has opened a very popular hair salon.
4. The Big Bad Wolf, whose famous fangs are the envy of canines everywhere, is appearing in a toothpaste commercial.
5. The cow, who recently appeared in a milk advertisement, jumped over the moon.
6. The dish, which is made of the finest porcelain, ran away with the spoon.

Answer Key

page 49, Goldilocks and the Commas

Goldilocks and the Three Bears

A little girl named Goldilocks was gathering flowers in the woods. She spotted a cottage and sneaked inside. She ate three bowls of porridge, sat in three different chairs, and tried out three different beds. She fell asleep in the last one. Presently, the three bears who lived in the cottage returned home.

"Someone has been eating my porridge," said Papa Bear.

"It appears," said Mama Bear, "that someone tasted mine as well."

Baby Bear shrieked, "Someone snarfed down my whole bowl!"

"Someone has been sitting in my chair," said Papa Bear.

"It seems," said Mama Bear, "that someone sat in mine as well."

Baby Bear screamed, "Oh man! My chair is broken to bits!"

"Someone has been sleeping in my bed," said Papa Bear.

"It is clear," said Mama Bear, "that someone slept in mine as well."

Baby Bear howled, "Some strange girl is sleeping in my bed!"

"Aaaaaaaagh," shrieked Goldilocks, waking up to the sight of the bears.

She ran out of the house, through the woods, and never returned to the cottage again.

QUOTATIONS

page 51, The Tortoise and the Hare

"I am so incredibly fast," bragged Hare.

"I'm unbelievably fast," bragged Tortoise.

Hare said, "Don't blink or you might miss me."

Tortoise said, "Don't get confused. You could easily mistake my shell for a speeding Indy car!"

"Enough of this, boys," said Skunk.

Skunk had been chosen as the referee. He said, "On your mark . . . get set . . . go!"

Hare and Tortoise were truly as fast as they claimed. But neither ran in the right direction.

Chipmunk shouted to Hare, "You're running in circles!"

Snail warned Tortoise, "You're going the wrong way!"

"This race is terrible," said Otter.

Owl had slept through most of the race. She woke up and asked, "Who's winning?"

"Who knows and who cares?" Raccoon replied.

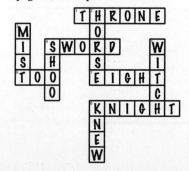

The moral of the story: "Those who boast need help the most."

page 52, Talking Princess Doll

1. At snack time she says, "I demand carrots!"
2. At bedtime she says, "I need some royal shut-eye."
3. "My castle is your castle," she says to guests.
4. "I'm going skateboarding," she says when she wants to play outside.
5. "Who is that handsome frog?" she asks when she spies a dashing amphibian.
6. If you keep pulling her string, she might even scream, "Stop pulling my string!"

page 53, Quotation Match

1. "I'll huff and I'll puff," said the Big Bad Wolf, "and I'll blow your house down!"
2. "You must be home by midnight," said the Fairy Godmother, "or your carriage will turn into a pumpkin."
3. "I wonder," said Baby Bear, "who's been eating my porridge."
4. "Since no one helped me," said the Little Red Hen, "I'll just eat the bread all by myself!"

APOSTROPHES

page 55, Crunch Time

1. I'm	3. You're	5. I'd	7. I've
2. It's	4. I'll	6. aren't	8. let's

page 56, Who's the Owner?

1. The Three Bears' porridge
2. King Midas's golden hamburger
3. The Three Little Pigs' houses
4. The queen's magic mirror
5. Tortoise's running shoes
6. Goldilocks's blonde hair
7. Rapunzel's extra-long hair
8. Bremen Town Musicians' instruments
9. Elves' miniature workshop
10. Little Red Riding Hood's picnic basket
11. Little Red Hen's loaf of bread
12. Troll's bridge

page 57, The Emperor's New Tinfoil Ball

Once upon a time there lived a very greedy emperor. He loved new stuff. He wasn't content with just a few new things. No matter how much he owned, he still couldn't be satisfied.

He didn't use his new stuff at all. Instead, he'd simply hide it away in a huge storage room. The emperor had the only key to the room, and it was made of gold.

One day a salesman paid a visit to the emperor's palace. "The King of Persia's most valuable possession can now be yours," said the salesman, holding up a ball of tinfoil. The salesman turned the ball so that the tinfoil's surface sparkled in the light. The emperor admired the glittering orb.

"It's priceless," said the salesman. "I'll trade it for that key." The emperor tore the key off its chain and handed it to him. He snatched the ball from the salesman's hand and rushed off to put it in his special storage room. When he arrived, he realized he didn't have the key anymore. The emperor's newest prize was now his only prize: a tinfoil ball.

HOMOPHONES

page 59, There, Their

1. The answer was provided as a model.
2. read, New
3. know, wear
4. one, too
5. through, right
6. bored, to, aloud
7. Hey, Hare
8. beat, tale
9. would, hear, night
10. Which, they're

page 60, Homophone Puzzler

```
              T H R O N E
  M           O
  I     S W O R D       W
  S     H     S         I
  T O O H     E I G H T C
  O     O               C
            K N I G H T H
            N
            E
            W
```